# ANNIE
# OAKLEY
## AMERICAN SHARPSHOOTER

SPECIAL LIVES IN HISTORY THAT BECOME

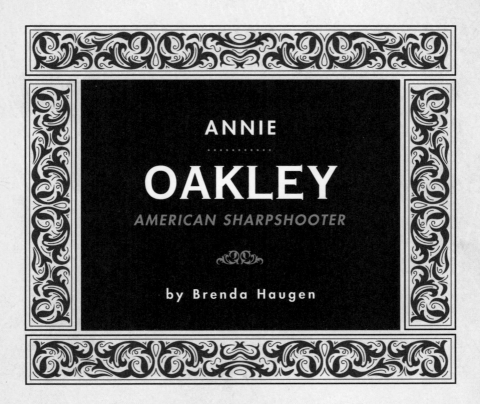

# ANNIE

# OAKLEY

*AMERICAN SHARPSHOOTER*

by Brenda Haugen

Content Adviser: Paul Fees, Ph.D.,
Consulting Curator, The Annie Oakley Center
Garst Museum, Greenville, Ohio

Reading Adviser: Rosemary G. Palmer, Ph.D.,
Department of Literacy, College of Education,
Boise State University

Compass Point Books ✦ Minneapolis, Minnesota

Compass Point Books
3109 West 50th Street, #115
Minneapolis, MN 55410

Visit Compass Point Books on the Internet at *www.compasspointbooks.com*
or e-mail your request to *custserv@compasspointbooks.com*

Editors: Sue Vander Hook, Mari Bolte
Page Production: Noumenon Creative
Photo Researchers: Lori Bye and Abbey Fitzgerald
Cartographer: XNR Productions, Inc.
Library Consultant: Kathleen Baxter

Art Director: Jaime Martens
Creative Director: Keith Griffin
Editorial Director: Carol Jones
Managing Editor: Catherine Neitge

*Special thanks to Lenn Sandahl for his help with this book. BLH*

**Library of Congress Cataloging-in-Publication Data**
Haugen, Brenda.
  Annie Oakley : American sharpshooter / by Brenda Haugen.
    p. cm. – (Signature lives)
  Includes bibliographical references and index.
  ISBN-13: 978-0-7565-1869-1 (library binding)
  ISBN-10: 0-7565-1869-5 (library binding)
  ISBN-13: 978-0-7565-1974-2 (paperback)
  ISBN-10: 0-7565-1974-8 (paperback)
1. Oakley, Annie, 1860-1926–Juvenile literature. 2. Shooters of
firarms–United States–Biography–Juvenile literature. 3. Women
entertainers–United States–Biography–Juvenile literature. I. Title. II. Series.
  GV1157.O3H27 2007
  799.3'092--dc22          2006027068
  [B]

*Signature Lives*

# MODERN AMERICA

Starting in the late 19th century, advancements in all areas of human activity transformed an old world into a new and modern place. Inventions prompted rapid shifts in lifestyle, and scientific discoveries began to alter the way humanity viewed itself. Beginning with World War I, warfare took place on a global scale, and ideas such as nationalism and communism showed that countries were taking a larger view of their place in the world. The combination of all these changes continues to produce what we know as the modern world.

Annie Oakley

# Table of Contents

# 1 SHARPSHOOTER AND LADY

❧❦❧

Annie Oakley blew kisses to the cheering crowd as she entered the arena. With a big smile, she bowed and waved while she hurried to center stage. There she stopped at a table on which her guns were neatly laid out and arranged.

After joining Buffalo Bill's Wild West show in 1885, Oakley had made a name for herself as one of the best shots around. Some who came to the Wild West show were surprised by her appearance. They expected the gun-toting Oakley to be rough, vulgar, and somewhat masculine. Instead, they discovered she was sweet and feminine.

While her personality was big, Oakley's body was small. She stood 5 feet (152.5 centimeters) tall and weighed 110 pounds (50 kilograms). Unlike the more

*Annie Oakley, popular star of Buffalo Bill's Wild West show, designed and sewed her own costumes.*

bawdy female performers of her day, Oakley dressed in modest but beautiful Western costumes that she designed and sewed herself. She embroidered flowers on her skirt and stitched ribbon trim along the hemline. From her knees to the top of her black shoes, she wore leggings. Her appearance was perfect—no wrinkles and no mistakes. She was just as she appeared—a lady.

Oakley presented an act the audience wouldn't soon forget. Oohs and aahs escaped from the crowd as she shot the ash from a cigarette dangling from her partner's mouth. Then from 90 feet (27 meters) away, Oakley hit the thin edge of a playing card and punctured it with five more holes before it hit the ground.

*Oakley used glass balls as targets in her shooting exhibitions. However, the shattered glass made such a mess that she soon switched to targets made of glazed clay.*

But Oakley saved her most amazing tricks for last. She ended her act by using a rifle and five shotguns to break 11 glass balls in 10 seconds. As her partner threw the balls into the air one by one, Oakley broke the first with a rifle shot. She quickly picked up a shotgun and used both barrels

## BUFFALO BILL'S WILD WEST·
### CONGRESS, ROUGH RIDERS OF THE WORLD.

### MISS ANNIE OAKLEY,
#### THE PEERLESS LADY WING-SHOT.

*A poster from Buffalo Bill's Wild West show featured Oakley wearing her many medals. In the background, Oakley was shooting glass balls as they were thrown into the air.*

to shatter the next two balls.

With lightning speed, she repeated the feat with shotgun after shotgun until all the balls were broken. After placing the last smoking gun back on the table, Oakley blew kisses to the crowd and ran off, giving her trademark little kick just before she left

William Frederick
"Buffalo Bill" Cody
(1846–1917) started
Buffalo Bill's Wild
West in Omaha,
Nebraska, in 1883. For
30 years, this spectacu-
lar outdoor traveling
show went from city
to city in the United
States and Europe.
As many as 1,200
performers re-enacted
Western events such as
the Pony Express,
buffalo hunts, stage-
coach robberies, and
attacks on wagon
trains. Each show
began with a parade
of colorfully costumed
entertainers on horse-
back. Sharpshooters,
cowboys, soldiers, and
Indians wowed audi-
ences with their thrill-
ing acts that offered a
taste of the Western
frontier.

the arena. Amazed at the act they had just witnessed, the audience cheered wildly and clapped.

At the height of her career in the late 1800s and early 1900s, Oakley reigned as one of the most famous women in the United States and perhaps the world. As a headliner in Buffalo Bill's Wild West, she dazzled everyone from common folk to royalty with her marksmanship and charm. She once said:

> *I have met the enthusiastic shooters of different lands, from the titled nobleman to the person occupying the humblest station in life, and, too, from the lady of royal blood to the rancher's daughter.*

With her talent and sparkling personality, Oakley brought them together and entertained them all. Although her performance only lasted 10 minutes, she made a lasting impression on her audience. With her femininity and skill at shooting, she showed that women could be more than assistants or pretty

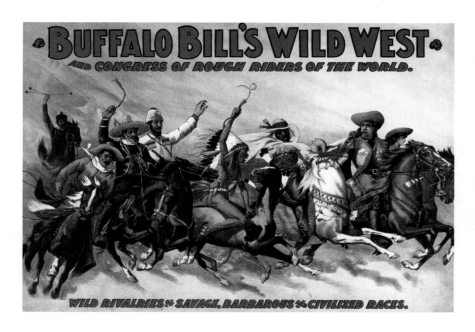

**BUFFALO BILL'S WILD WEST**

AND CONGRESS OF ROUGH RIDERS OF THE WORLD.

WILD RIVALRIES OF SAVAGE, BARBAROUS AND CIVILIZED RACES.

bystanders. She demonstrated that a woman could participate in what were considered men's activities and still be very much a lady. Her athletic endeavors made shooting and hunting more acceptable activities for women.

This sharpshooter, who came to be known as Little Sure Shot, would gain fame in a man's world. She would bring the spirit of the Old West to audiences worldwide and capture people's hearts along the way.

*The "Congress of Rough Riders" in Buffalo Bill's Wild West allowed cowboys, cowgirls, Indians, and horsemen of many nations and races to compete as equals in the arena.*

# 2 GROWING UP QUICKLY

❧✦❧

When Annie Oakley was born on August 13, 1860, her parents named her Phoebe Ann Moses. Her three older sisters called her Annie. She would be 21 years old before she would begin using the stage name Annie Oakley.

Annie was born in Patterson Township in northern Darke County, Ohio. Her parents, Jacob and Susan Moses, had moved there from Pennsylvania in 1855 after a fire destroyed the inn where they worked. Jacob and Susan decided to make a fresh start in Ohio with their three daughters. The family cleared a plot of land, and Jacob built a cabin from trees he cut down himself.

After the move, two more daughters were born to Jacob and Susan, but one died before she was a

*Phoebe Ann Moses was born in the house her father built in western Ohio. She lived there until she was 8 years old.*

year old. Then Annie, their sixth daughter, was born. When she was 2, a baby brother named John joined the family. Two years later, another sister, Hulda, completed the Moses family.

Annie liked spending time with her father and brother more than playing dolls with her sisters. She enjoyed wandering through the nearby woods and tracking animals. Her father taught her how to make traps out of cornstalks to catch wild game.

The Moses children were hard workers. As soon as they were old enough to help, they were assigned chores. They fed the animals, fixed fences, gathered wild berries, helped with housework, and worked in the fields. It was difficult and time-consuming work, and as a result, the children didn't have time to go to school.

Susan canned and dried fruits and vegetables to make sure her large family would have food during the winter. Jacob butchered cows in the fall, smoked the meat, and used the cowhide to make shoes for his family.

During the winter, Jacob took his crops to the mill in town about 14 miles (22 kilometers) away. He would also stop at the general store to buy supplies for the winter months. In 1865, on the way home from one of those trips, Jacob got caught in a blizzard. The weather had been clear earlier that day when he loaded his horse-drawn wagon with corn and wheat.

But on the drive home, the weather took a turn for the worse. Bitter cold and savage winds whipped up the snow, making it difficult for him to see.

By midnight, Jacob still had not made it home. Five-year-old Annie waited anxiously with the rest of her family for her father to return. Because the blizzard's blowing snow blocked their view of the road, Susan and her children heard Jacob's wagon before they saw it. Relieved Jacob was home, they all ran out in the frigid night to greet him.

Annie remembered, "Mother threw the door wide open into the face of the howling wind." The sight nearly took their breath away. There sat Jacob "with the reins around his neck and wrists, for his dear

*Farmers like Jacob Moses depended on the land to supply their families with food and income.*

**17**

hands had been frozen so he could not use them. His speech was gone." Susan and her oldest daughter, Mary Jane, helped Jacob into the house. Annie and the other children unhooked the horses from the wagon and got them into the barn.

Susan tried to nurse her husband back to health, but a few weeks later, in early 1866, Jacob Moses died of pneumonia. Susan, 33, was now a widow with seven children. The following year, tragedy struck again. Mary Jane died of tuberculosis, and Susan was forced to sell the children's pet cow, Pink, to pay for the medical and funeral expenses. They could no longer afford their farm, so they moved to a smaller farm that a kind neighbor allowed Susan and her family to rent.

*A photograph believed by some to be Susan Moses, Annie Oakley's mother*

Life was not easy for the Moses family. With Jacob and Mary Jane gone, all the daily work of running the farm fell to Susan and her six remaining children. Since they couldn't afford to hire outside help, the entire family worked hard all day.

But life was not all work for the Moses family. Annie's mother set aside a special block of time each evening to spend with her children. The family belonged to a religious group called the Quakers, and Susan made sure her children learned to trust in God, to work hard, and to always be honest. Annie would later remember these times with her mother:

> But every night, ... no matter how tired we all were, mother washed our hands and feet, brushed and plaited our hair into pigtails, took little John and Baby Huldie onto her lap, and sang hymns with us and prayed God to watch over us.

Although Annie and her family were hard workers, there was still never enough to eat. Annie decided to help put food on the table. At about age 6, she put her trapping skills to work and headed into the woods. Nearly every day, she caught several small birds with cornstalk traps, just like her father had taught her. The birds were lured to the traps by corn

*Commonly known as the Quakers, the Religious Society of Friends was founded in England in the 1600s. George Fox (1624–1691) played a major role in forming this religious group that was dissatisfied with existing Christian religions. Quakers believe that all people can have a personal experience with God. They obey what they call the Inner Light within, which they believe comes directly from God. William Penn (1644–1718) founded the colony of Pennsylvania as a safe haven for Quakers who were being oppressed in other colonies. He called Pennsylvania his Holy Experiment.*

that Annie placed in a trench underneath the traps. Susan eagerly cooked everything Annie caught, and the entire family gratefully ate it.

Annie wanted to use her father's rifle to shoot game, but her mother wouldn't allow it. She worried that Annie might hurt herself. However, her mother eventually relented. Annie would later recall:

> *I was eight years old when I took my first shot, and I still consider it one of the best shots I ever made. ... I saw a squirrel run down over the grass in front of the house, through the orchard and stop on a fence to get a hickory nut.*

Annie ran into the house, climbed on a chair, and took down her father's rifle from its place of honor above the fireplace mantle. She took the gun outside, rested the barrel on the porch railing, aimed at a squirrel, and pulled the trigger. "It was a wonderful shot," she said, "going right through the head from side to side." Annie knew the importance of making a precise shot. Not only did the shot kill the animal instantly and prevent further suffering, it also ensured that the most meat possible would be saved for eating.

In spite of Annie's ability to provide extra meat for the table, Susan still couldn't support her large family. The $1.25 a week she earned as a district

*Hunting remained one of Annie Oakley's favorite activities throughout her life.*

health nurse didn't cover all their expenses. Susan was forced to make a difficult decision. She accepted help from friends and neighbors who offered to take some of her children. Susan's friend Nancy Edington agreed to care for Annie. ❧

# 3 HELPING HER FAMILY

⤜⤚✤⤙⤛

Eight-year-old Annie didn't want to leave her home and family, but she realized her mother had no choice. Annie went to live nearby with Samuel and Nancy Edington, superintendents of the Darke County Infirmary—the county poor farm. The large three-story brick building on the south side of Greenville, Ohio, housed children and adults alike, from the poor and orphans to people who were mentally ill and couldn't care for themselves on their own.

The Edingtons lived at the infirmary, although they were separate from the residents. The Edingtons were kind to Annie and treated her like their own daughter. Nancy taught Annie to knit, embroider, and use a sewing machine. With her new skills, Annie was able to make money sewing uniforms and quilts and

*The Darke County Infirmary was built in 1856 for people who were homeless or needed residential care.*

*Annie Oakley learned to embroider as a young child. She would later embroider beautiful designs on her own clothes and costumes.*

patching clothes for residents of the infirmary.

After Annie had been with the Edingtons for a few weeks, a man asked to hire Annie. He wanted her to help care for his 3-week-old boy while his wife cared for the house and the older children. In those days, it wasn't unusual for poor children to be hired out to work in homes. With her mother's permission, Annie went to live with the couple she would later refer to only as the "he-wolf" and "she-wolf." The man promised Annie she would have time to hunt and go to school. He also promised to send 50 cents a week to her mother.

At first, the job went well. However, after Annie had been with the family about a month, they began treating her like a slave. Annie said:

> *I got up at 4 o'clock in the morning, got breakfast, milked the cows, washed dishes, skimmed milk, fed the calves and pigs, pumped the water for the cattle, fed the chickens, rocked the baby to sleep, weeded the garden, picked wild blackberries and got dinner. ... Mother wrote for me to come home. But they would not let me go. I was held a prisoner.*

They quickly forgot their promise to let Annie get an education. The couple regularly wrote to Susan and lied that Annie was doing well in school. They also physically abused Annie. Although she would never share the details, she had permanent proof of her abuse—welts and scars on her back.

Annie did tell one story about her time with the family. Tired from a long day of hard work, she had fallen asleep while mending a stocking. The woman she called she-wolf punished Annie by forcing her outside into the snow with no shoes and locking her out of the house. Annie remembered:

*I was slowly freezing to death. ... So I got down on my little knees, looked toward God's clear sky, and tried to pray. But my lips were frozen stiff and there was no sound.*

When the she-wolf saw her husband coming home, she quickly took Annie back into the house and warmed her by the fire. Annie bravely withstood the abuse because she believed they were sending money to her family. But after working for them for nearly two years, Annie could stand it no longer. When the couple wasn't at home, Annie left and headed to the nearby railroad station. A kind man listened to her story and paid her fare. She boarded a train, got off near Woodland, and walked the rest of the way to her mother's house.

Things had changed while Annie was away. Her mother had married a man named Daniel Brumbaugh, and they had a child named Emily. But Brumbaugh had died, and Susan now had a third husband, Joseph Shaw. They lived in a home near North Star, not far from Woodland.

Susan and Joseph both welcomed Annie home. Annie, however, quickly realized that neither her mother nor Joseph was in good health, and they were barely scraping by financially. She went back to the Edingtons, where she could work and send extra money to her needy family.

The man Annie called he-wolf came looking for her, but the Edingtons wouldn't let him take her. Nancy Edington had seen Annie's scarred back, and she told her husband and son to throw the man out and warn him never to come back. "That night ... I slept untroubled for the first time in long months," Annie wrote.

*In the 1860s, people often traveled by train. Annie probably rode on the Baltimore and Ohio railway when she went to Woodland, Ohio, to see her mother.*

Annie began earning money as a seamstress. She also learned how to read and write, sometimes in a classroom and other times by following along as the Edingtons read aloud in the evenings. She worked more than she went to school. She was such a responsible worker that the Edingtons put her in charge of the infirmary's dairy. She milked 12 cows, skimmed cream, and made butter for the kitchen. This job paid more money, which allowed Annie to buy Christmas gifts for her family for the first time in her life. She also sewed fancy cuffs and collars to brighten the dark dresses the infirmary orphans wore. She was always one who brought sunshine into the lives of others.

Annie spent the next few years with the Edingtons and then with her own family once again. Although she worked hard and always worried about money, Annie was happy with her life. Whenever she lived with her mother, she learned to be frugal. With

*Farmers worked hard to make a living for themselves and their families.*

limited resources, her mother didn't waste any food and made sure to use every scrap of spare fabric. Annie again helped supply food for the table by hunting and trapping game. She sold the game to the owners of the Katzenberger brothers' grocery store in Greenville. The storekeepers then sold her meat to hotels and restaurants in nearby cities, including Cincinnati about 80 miles (128 km) away.

When Susan and Joseph's mortgage on their house had to be paid, Annie gave them money she had earned from selling game. Although she was barely a teenager, Annie was able to give her mother enough money to pay off the entire debt on her house. This gave Annie great joy.

In the mid-1870s, the situation improved for Annie's family. Two of her older sisters married and moved out to start families of their own, which eased the financial burden on the family. Sometime before Thanksgiving in 1875, 15-year-old Annie went to visit her sister Lydia and her husband, Joe Stein, in Fairmount, Ohio, a suburb of Cincinnati. Little did Annie know that the trip would change her life. ✑

> *Today, about 13,000 people live in the city of Greenville, Ohio. It's the home of the Darke County Fair, which began in 1853. Also in Greenville is the Annie Oakley Center at the Garst Museum. On display are artifacts and exhibits that give an account of Oakley's life. A statue of Oakley is proudly displayed in the Annie Oakley Memorial Park, honoring the famous markswoman who grew up in the area.*

# 4 A CHALLENGE AND A COURTSHIP

☙❦❧

In Cincinnati, Annie met a man named Frank Butler. He had made a name for himself as an excellent marksman and traveled around the United States giving shooting exhibitions. He was in Cincinnati in November 1875 to perform his act at an arena called the Coliseum.

On occasion, Butler accepted challenges from local sharpshooters who thought they could outshoot him. So he wasn't surprised when a Cincinnati man approached him with a challenge.

Jack Frost, a hotel owner, told Butler he knew of someone from Ohio who could beat him in a shooting match. Frost was willing to wager $100 if Butler would take the challenge. Needing the money, Butler laughed and accepted, although sometimes

*Annie Oakley, Frank Butler, and his dog, George, posed for a publicity shot.*

he felt a little guilty about taking what he thought was easy money from foolish people.

Then Butler found out his competition was a 15-year-old girl named Annie Moses. Frost had often bought game from Annie and knew how talented she was with a gun. Although accounts surrounding the match between Annie and Butler vary, everyone agrees on the outcome—young Annie Moses was a better shot than Frank Butler, the man who made his living as an expert marksman and trick-shooter.

Butler now realized that Annie Moses was no joke—she was a natural markswoman. He said:

> *I was a beaten man the moment she appeared for I was taken off guard. ... Never were the birds so hard for two shooters as they flew from us, but never did a person make more impossible shots than did that little girl. She killed 23 and I killed 21. It was her first big match—my first defeat.*

After the match, Butler invited Annie and her family to his exhibition at the Cincinnati Coliseum. They accepted the invitation, and Butler gave them free passes.

At Butler's show, Annie was fascinated by his dog, a poodle named George. As part of his act, Butler shot an apple off George's head. Then George picked up a piece of the apple with his mouth and dropped

Cincinnati, Ohio, was a busy river port founded in 1788. By the 1870s it was a well-established city.

it at Annie's feet. It was the start of Annie's longtime admiration of George. But it was also the beginning of Butler and Annie's friendship, which would soon become a romance.

Butler was smitten by the pretty young shooter, and he didn't forget about her after he left to perform in other towns. Taking advantage of Annie's fondness of George, Butler often sent notes and candy to her, all in George's name.

Annie and Butler had a great deal in common. Both were excellent shooters, but more important, they shared many of the same values. Neither smoked, drank, or gambled. They also had both survived difficult childhoods. When Butler was 8 years old, his poverty-stricken parents in Ireland had left him with one of his aunts. At the age of 13, he left his homeland and sailed to the United States, where he got an education and worked to support himself.

Annie's family, however, had some concerns about her relationship with Butler. He was 10 years older than Annie. He had also been married, had a child, and was divorced. In those days, divorce was unacceptable to many people.

But her family gave in when they saw how much he loved Annie and how well he treated her. Although historians don't agree on

*Francis "Frank" Butler (1850–1926) grew up in Ireland, one of the poorest countries in Europe at that time. Most of the people who lived there toiled on small farms and depended on potato crops for their every-day existence. In the mid-1840s, the potato crop was struck with a fungus that spread from one place to another. Soon there were no potato crops to harvest, and the country was swept up in a famine. It took many years for Ireland to recover. During that time, nearly a million Irish people immigrated to the United States and Canada to find better lives.*

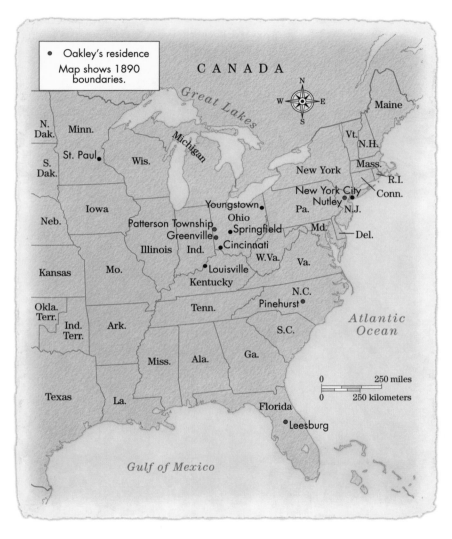

the exact date, Butler and Annie were most likely married on August 23, 1876.

Now Annie lived life on the road with Butler as he traveled from show to show. She wasn't part of the act, but she wouldn't be a spectator for long. ✦

*Annie Oakley was born in Ohio and spent years traveling throughout the country during her career.*

# 5 "ANNIE OAKLEY" IS BORN

*Chapter*

❧⟨❀⟩❧

Frank Butler was scheduled to perform with his partner at Crystal Hall in Springfield, Ohio, on May 1, 1882. But when his partner got sick, Butler asked Annie to help out. He wanted her to be his assistant and to hold objects as he shot them. Annie agreed to help, but she wanted to be more than just an assistant. She insisted on taking every other shot. Butler agreed.

Their show was such a hit and so much fun for both of them that they decided to tour together. Annie wanted to choose a stage name to use on the entertainment circuit. Historians are not sure why, but the name she chose was Annie Oakley. The act was called "Butler and Oakley."

With the help of her husband, Annie Oakley

*Sitting Bull, a Lakota Indian chief, would eventually adopt Annie Oakley into the tribe as his daughter.*

*Before becoming a popular marksman, Frank Butler cleaned stables and managed an on-stage dog show.*

worked to build her reading and writing skills as the couple traveled across the country. Butler also helped her come up with new tricks to improve their show. Oakley was now earning enough to start saving money in the bank. Though Oakley was never wasteful with her money, she did like to buy fancy hair ribbons and gloves for herself.

Oakley also sent money to her mother and visited her every chance she got. Susan was proud of her daughter, who stuck to her Quaker values. Though indecent shows were gaining popularity, Oakley refused to dress scantily or wear makeup. She used her sewing skills to make modest costumes for herself. She wanted her show to be suitable for families. Her husband shared her values.

Those standards drew the attention of Lakota Indian chief and holy man Sitting Bull. Even though his home was at Fort Yates, South Dakota, on the Standing Rock Reservation, Sitting Bull traveled occasionally. In March 1884, he visited St. Paul,

Minnesota, and watched one of Oakley and Butler's shows. Oakley said:

> He was about as much taken by my shooting stunts as anyone ever has been. ... He raved about me. ... His messengers kept coming down to my hotel to enquire if I would come and see him. I had other things to do, and could not spare the time.

Sitting Bull requested a meeting with Oakley several times, but each time she politely refused. She was too busy preparing for her next show. Finally,

*A publicity poster showed Oakley shooting glass balls while standing on the back of a galloping horse.*

*Sitting Bull, a Hunkpapa Lakota chief and holy man, was born around 1831 in present-day South Dakota. His courage became legendary as stories circulated about him calmly sitting and enjoying a pipe with friends as bullets flew around him. He also served as a leader in the crushing defeat of U.S. General George Custer in the Battle of the Little Bighorn. After eluding the U.S. military for years, Sitting Bull finally surrendered in 1881 and submitted to living on a reservation.*

Sitting Bull sent a messenger to her hotel to give her $65 and to ask for a photo. Oakley sent the money back to him, along with her picture.

The next morning, the two finally met. They liked each other right away and became lifelong friends. Sitting Bull fondly called Oakley Watanya Cicilla, which means "Little Sure Shot." He also insisted on adopting Annie, making her forever welcome in his home and a part of his family. He said that she reminded him of his daughter who had died years before. Oakley took the adoption so seriously that she would later label a photograph of Sitting Bull "Adopted Father of Annie Oakley."

Oakley didn't realize what an honor Sitting Bull's adoption was until later in her life. She knew she'd never go to the Dakota Territory to take what now was rightfully hers as a daughter of a Lakota chief. But she could have claimed horses, cattle, and property. Butler saw great value in his wife's friendship with Sitting Bull. He used their relationship to promote Oakley as a true woman of the American West.

Later in 1884, Oakley and Butler signed a 40-week contract to join the Sells Brothers Circus. At that time, circuses often included shooting acts. Many people owned guns for protection or hunting and enjoyed seeing what professional marksmen could do with their weapons. However, Oakley and Butler wanted to stand out from the crowd and do more than just the same old tricks other marksmen were

*The Sells Brothers Circus ran from 1871 to 1911. It eventually became part of the Ringling Brothers, Barnum and Bailey's Greatest Show on Earth.*

doing. They came up with the idea of shooting while riding on a horse. The circus crowds loved it.

Life with the circus was hard, though. In 1884, the Sells Brothers Circus traveled about 11,000 miles (17,600 km) and played in 187 cities in 13 states, including Ohio, Illinois, Texas, and Arkansas. The troupe often traveled every day, rain or shine. When it rained, conditions were miserable, and many in the troupe became ill. They weren't fed very well, and sometimes they weren't paid on time.

However, Oakley and Butler were so popular with audiences that the circus agreed to pay them more if they would sign a contract for another year. The couple agreed to come back the next season. In the meantime, they needed to find work during the winter when the circus wasn't performing.

In early December, Butler saw an ad for a show called Buffalo Bill's Wild West. The show was scheduled to open in New Orleans, Louisiana, on December 8. The Sells Brothers Circus' last performance of the season happened to be in the same city on December 15. Oakley and Butler hoped at least one of them would be hired for the Buffalo Bill show.

But Buffalo Bill Cody, the owner of the show, refused to hire either Oakley or Butler. His show already boasted a fine array of excellent marksmen, including Captain Adam Bogardus, a world-cham-

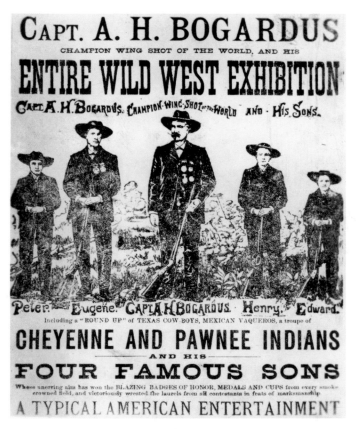

*Captain Adam Bogardus, one of the country's most famous marksmen, was the inventor of the glass balls Annie used as targets in her act.*

pion shooter. He and his four sons were the stars of the show.

The disappointed Butlers decided to head north, where they worked in a variety of theaters and lived in boardinghouses. However, they would soon get another chance to become part of Buffalo Bill's Wild West show. ᕉ

## Chapter 6
# BUFFALO BILL'S WILD WEST

᠅

Oakley and Butler knew that if Buffalo Bill Cody would give them a chance, they would become a valuable part of his show. When Bogardus left the show in March 1885, Oakley and Butler wasted no time approaching Cody. They offered to give three free performances to show their worth. Cody finally gave in and agreed that the couple could audition that spring in Louisville, Kentucky.

Oakley spent weeks practicing at a trapshooting range in Cincinnati. Not wanting to fail at this opportunity, she worked hard to sharpen her skills. On the day of the audition in Louisville, the Wild West grounds were deserted except for one man who had wandered in and hung around the grandstands. Butler suggested that Oakley use the time to practice her

*Before starting his Wild West show, Buffalo Bill Cody was a trapper, Pony Express rider, stagecoach driver, Civil War soldier, and hotel manager.*

act. When she finished, the man in the grandstands ran up to the Butlers and hired them on the spot. The man was Cody's business partner, Nate Salsbury.

Cody introduced Oakley and Butler to the rest of the group, which included cowboys, Native

*The Wild West troupe included former cowboys, Indians, Pony Express riders, sharpshooters, musicians, stagecoach drivers, and more. Annie Oakley was standing in the second row, third from the right. Buffalo Bill Cody was seated in the first row, third from the left.*

Americans, Mexicans, and a variety of people from his staff. Oakley recalled, "There I was facing the real Wild West, the first white woman to travel with what society might have considered an impossible outfit."

Cody told his crew, "This little Missie here is Miss

*Buffalo Bill Cody was nicknamed for his skill at hunting buffalo. Buffalo is the common term for bison, a large, hairy animal with a massive head and shoulders and a humped back. A male bison, called a bull, can grow to 6 feet (180 cm) tall at the hump and weigh more than 2,000 pounds (900 kg). Huge herds of buffalo once roamed the Plains, but they were hunted nearly to extinction. Today, about 300,000 bison live on ranches in the United States and Canada. There are also free-roaming herds in parks and preserves around the country, like Yellowstone National Park which is home to more than 2,000 bison. Although bison are raised mainly for their meat, their hides are used to make everything from shoes to blankets.*

Annie Oakley. She's to be the only white woman with our show. And I want you boys to welcome her and protect her." Everyone was friendly and happy to meet the Butlers. Then the sound of a trumpet called the entertainers to the mess tent so they could all eat together.

"So began my life with the B.B.W.W. [Buffalo Bill's Wild West]," Oakley later said. Joining the Wild West show marked a change in how Oakley and Butler's act was advertised. In the past, Butler received top billing or the couple shared the limelight. With the Sells Brothers Circus, the couple had been marketed together as champion rifle shots. But with the Wild West show, Oakley was the star. Her name and phrases such as "A Special Feature" or "Champion Markswoman" were on the posters.

Butler now happily worked as his wife's assistant and manager. During Oakley's performances, he loaded traps with targets called clay pigeons. When Butler released

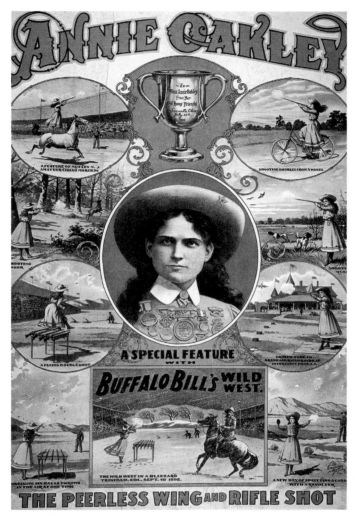

A 1901 poster advertising Buffalo Bill's Wild West show featured Annie Oakley as "The Peerless Wing and Rifle Shot."

the clay device from the trap, flinging it into the sky, Oakley quickly shattered it with her shotgun. She could shoot as many as four clay pigeons in the air, one after the other.

After wowing the crowd with trapshooting,

Oakley used pistols or a rifle to shoot glass balls that were thrown into the air by another troupe member. For a finale, she threw the balls into the air herself, picked up her gun from the ground, and shot them before they fell to the ground. Audiences were amazed. The deafening sound of applause escorted Oakley out of the arena as she bowed and blew kisses to the crowd.

Many people didn't know Oakley and Butler were married since they had different last names. But that didn't bother Butler. Instead of being jealous of his wife's success, he was one of her many admirers. He gladly helped his wife become a better performer. They worked together to improve her act. He served as her press agent, scheduling newspaper interviews for her and promoting her performances. And he also handled her mail and managed her money.

During the Butlers' first season with the Wild West show, Oakley performed about halfway through the show. For each performance, she skipped into the arena and blew kisses to the crowd. Her long hair hung down her back, and she wore a loose blouse, a knee-length skirt, leggings, and a cowboy hat. She wore the outfit not only out of modesty but also because it gave her the freedom she needed to make quick movements during her performance. Oakley's grace, beauty, and sweetness helped make those who were skittish about the noisy gunshots more at ease. Her demeanor helped attract many women and children to the Wild West shows. One fan recalled:

> *Her entrance was always a very pretty one.*
> *She never walked. She tripped in, bowing,*
> *waving, and wafting kisses. Her first few*
> *shots brought forth a few screams of fright*
> *from the women, but they were soon lost*
> *in round after round of applause.*

Along with shooting performances, the Wild West show also gave its audiences a glimpse of the American frontier. The show included dramatic

*Annie Oakley and the Native American performers in Buffalo Bill's Wild West show*

enactments of buffalo hunts, stagecoach rescues, and Indian attacks on settlers' homes.

The first year traveling with the Wild West show was exhausting for Oakley, but she enjoyed it. The troupe journeyed through the central and eastern United States before going into Canada. The season ended in Youngstown, in eastern Ohio. The group usually traveled by train at night to each new destination. They used boards to connect seats across the aisles and plopped mattresses and blankets on them to form makeshift beds. The troupe rose at 5 A.M. each day to get ready for the next show.

When they weren't traveling, the Butlers stayed in their own tent that they set up on the performance grounds. Oakley bought two cots so she and Butler could sleep comfortably, and she decorated the tent to make it as homey as possible. It served as a retreat where she could embroider in her free time and entertain guests, which she loved to do.

Each morning, Oakley took a bath in a collapsible tub that she kept inside the tent. After getting dressed, she often ate a big breakfast of steak, fruit, bread, and coffee. She claimed that a hearty breakfast gave her the energy she needed for her busy day. Every day, Oakley practiced her act, took an afternoon nap, ate dinner, and then performed in the evening.

The Wild West show had a profitable year in 1885, earning nearly $100,000 (about $2 million

ANNIE
OAKLEY.

today). When the season closed, Oakley and Butler headed to Ohio to visit Oakley's mother and siblings. They'd do so, however, without George. Their beloved poodle had died when the troupe was in Ohio.

Oakley used the winter off-season to practice her reading and writing skills. She also spent time doing one of her favorite things: hunting. She practiced her act and worked with Butler to come up with new tricks for the next season. As she'd soon find out, though, others were jealous of her stardom and would be more than happy to take her place in the show if she should become unpopular. ᴥ

*When Annie Oakley traveled with Buffalo Bill's Wild West show, she decorated her tent with flowers and a picket fence.*

# 7 INTERNATIONAL STAR

〜✦〜

One of Annie Oakley's rivals was 15-year-old Lillian Smith, a newcomer who joined the act in 1886. Smith had no intention of sharing the spotlight with anyone else. She made no secret of her claim that she was better than Oakley. They quickly became opponents rather than friends. Oakley pushed herself even harder to maintain her spot as the Wild West's main shooting attraction.

That year, the troupe got a new, temporary home—an open-air arena at Erastina resort in New York City. The show would be based there throughout the summer. The 1886 season began with a parade in New York City. But on that day, Oakley was ill. Smith was more than willing to take her place, but Oakley refused to let her sickness keep her away.

Erastus Wiman, president of the Staten Island Amusement Company, built the Erastina resort in a wooded rural area of New York that was later called Staten Island. He built ballparks, casinos, and lavish restaurants, and organized huge entertainment spectacles. In 1886, he brought the popular Buffalo Bill's Wild West to Erastina for the summer.

She proudly rode on horseback along the 17-mile (27-km) parade route. However, she paid a high price. Back at Erastina, she bled five hours from an infection in her right ear. The next morning, a doctor diagnosed her with blood poisoning, the result of a bug flying into her ear. Oakley missed four days of work. This would be the only time in her 40-year career that she would miss a performance.

The Wild West show became a huge hit at Erastina. By the end of the first month, about 360,000 people had attended the show. People were turned away at the gate because there wasn't enough room to hold them all in the grandstands. Carpenters built an addition to the grandstands to hold larger crowds.

The following year, the Wild West troupe spent part of the season performing in New York's Madison Square Garden. The arena's roof had to be raised 25 feet (7.6 m) to accommodate the show, mainly because of the shooters' tricks. As usual, Oakley added new tricks to her repertoire. Among the most popular were those tricks that showcased her horseback riding skills. In one performance, she untied a handkerchief just above her horse's hoof as she rode at full speed hanging down from her sidesaddle. For her horsemanship, Oakley received a gold medal from the New York Ladies Riding Club. It would be one of many honors she would be awarded in her career.

On March 31, 1887, the Wild West crew and the show's animals—180 horses, 18 buffalo, 10 mules, and 10 elk—boarded a ship bound for London. They were on their way to be part of the celebration of Queen Victoria's Golden Jubilee. It was the 50th anniversary of her coronation as queen of England.

*The Wild West show performed in the festivities that commemorated the 50th anniversary of Victoria's reign as queen of England.*

Some of the troupe, particularly the Native Americans, were nervous about the ocean journey. Violent storms they encountered only increased their fears. But Oakley didn't appear bothered by the trip. In fact, she and her rival, Lillian Smith, kept up their practice schedules, sharpening their shooting skills on the deck of the ship.

The Wild West show opened in London on May 9, 1887. In the first three weeks, more than 500,000 people attended. Oakley met many dignitaries during her five-month stay. Among them were Edward, Prince of Wales, and his wife, Princess Alexandra. Oakley became friends with both of them. Prince Edward commented on Oakley: "What a pity there are not more women in the world like that little one."

*Princess Alexandra and the Prince of Wales, who later became Edward VII, king of England*

Others agreed. Of all the shooters in the show, Oakley gained the most attention from the public. Newspaper reporters wrote often about her feats. Everyone wanted to meet this charming, petite woman who could outshoot anyone, male or female. Oakley accepted invitations to dinner parties, balls, and teas. Her tent was filled with flowers and gifts from admirers. Her collection of medals, awards, and trophies continued to grow, and people recognized her wherever she went.

After the last show in London on October 31, 1887, Oakley and Butler left the Wild West show. Neither the Butlers nor Buffalo Bill Cody would ever say why. Some have speculated that Smith played a part in their leaving. Oakley may have complained to Cody about Smith's boastful behavior and more risqué way of dressing. When nothing changed, Oakley may have decided to leave the show.

The Butlers then traveled to Berlin, Germany, where they put on an exhibition at the Charlottenburg Race Course. Among the spectators was Germany's Crown Prince Wilhelm, whom Oakley saved from disaster. When an out-of-control horse headed toward him during the show, Oakley pushed the prince out of the way so he wouldn't be run over.

In 1888, Oakley and Butler returned to New York City and lived in an apartment across from Madison Square Garden. During her time in London, Oakley had given shooting lessons to women. In the United States, she continued giving lessons to any woman who was interested.

Oakley believed it was healthy for women to be outdoors and enjoy the beauty of nature. She believed

*Oakley (at rail, second from right), enjoyed teaching other women to shoot.*

shooting and hunting added to a woman's confidence. Oakley also thought women should know how to use weapons for their own protection.

However, she made it clear that outdoor sports were just a part of a well-rounded woman's life. Oakley said:

> *I do not wish to be understood to mean by this that woman should sacrifice home and family duties entirely merely for out-side pleasure but ... no opportunity should be lost ... in outdoor sports, pastimes, and recreations, which are at once healthy in their tone and results and womanly in their character.*

Butler got to work negotiating contracts for his wife. Among them was a stint with Tony Pastor's variety show. The show featured a wide array of acts, including singers, dancers, and comedians. While Oakley's act helped fill the seats, she didn't rank as the leading attraction in the show.

In her spare time, Oakley continued to give shooting exhibitions. Once thought of as a man's pastime, shooting demonstrations began gaining popularity with women. In fact, at Oakley's shows, about half the crowd was female. Some asked Oakley how she became such an expert shot. Oakley realized that in her case, she had a special talent. Practice helped, but that was only part of it. "I don't know how I acquired the skill," she answered. "I suppose I was born with it."

In July 1888, Oakley made her first appearance with Pawnee Bill Historical Wild West Exhibition and Indian Encampment. She played to a full grandstand in Gloucester Beach, New Jersey. Though she received top billing and was treated with respect, Oakley didn't like some of the acts. She was shocked when Pawnee Bill made a public spectacle of a Kaw Indian chief's wedding.

Meanwhile, Buffalo Bill and his partner, Nate Salsbury, didn't like Oakley working for a competing show. Whatever the differences were that had caused Oakley to leave the Wild West show, they apparently

CORRECT VIEW OF PAWNEE BILL'S WILD WEST, GIVEN IN A CANVAS INCLOSURE UNDER HEAVEN'S CANOPY, THE PUBLIC AMPLY PROTECTED FROM THE ELEMENTS.

*Pawnee Bill's Wild West show toured the world for 25 years, from 1888 to 1913. In its glory days the show had a crew of 645 people, more than 400 horses and steers, and 20 buffalo.*

were worked out. Perhaps Oakley returned because Lillian Smith was no longer with the show. In any case, Oakley left Pawnee Bill's show in August 1888. In early 1889, she joined Buffalo Bill's troupe, which was performing in Paris, France.

The French people loved Oakley. Along with sold-out performances and top billing, Oakley enjoyed invitations to dinner parties, balls, and meetings with royalty. The troupe stayed in Paris six months before taking the show to other parts of France, Italy, and Spain.

In Barcelona, Spain, several members of the group, including Oakley and Butler, became ill with the flu. It was quickly becoming a widespread epidemic. The show's announcer and several Native Americans died of the disease, but Oakley and Butler recovered.

However, rumors spread that Oakley had died, and newspapers in the United States picked up the story. Oakley's mother cried for two days thinking her daughter was dead. Then she discovered the story wasn't true. Butler put notices in American newspapers saying Oakley was alive and well. Oakley quickly wrote to friends, family, and fans to assure them she was fine.

Through the years, Buffalo Bill's Wild West show continued to make a profit, even when the economy in the United States declined. In 1893, the show earned nearly $1 million ($20 million today). Instead of being content with his success, Buffalo Bill worked to expand the show.

Oakley added new tricks and improved her showmanship. She trained her horse, Gipsy, to follow her up a flight of stairs and into a freight elevator. She also learned to shoot targets behind her back. She

> *Pawnee Bill's real name was Gordon W. Lillie. He went to Oklahoma at the age of 15 to teach the Pawnee Indians, who nicknamed him Pawnee Bill. In 1883, he left teaching to join Buffalo Bill's Wild West show, where he met and married May Manning. In 1888, he and his wife established their own show which re-enacted exciting adventures of the Western frontier. May Manning Lillie was a star of the show, performing as a markswoman and bronco rider. The show toured the world from 1888 through 1913.*

placed her rifle backward over her shoulder and used a mirror to accomplish this crowd-pleasing stunt.

The public and critics loved her. Cody knew it and paid her appropriately. Because there are no records, it is unknown how much she actually made. Oakley said that when she started performing with Buffalo Bill's Wild West she earned more than $100 per week ($2,000 today). This was the highest salary of any of the troupe members. As her fame grew, so

*Oakley was an accurate shot even when she fired over her shoulder.*

did her income. Though she had to pay for her own costumes, guns, and sometimes housing and food, Oakley realized how fortunate she was. The average worker in the United States at that time made less than $10 a week. When the Wild West troupe traveled by train, the Butlers had their own room, complete with a bed, dresser, and two comfortable chairs. They even had running water, which was quite a luxury in those days.

In the summer of 1893, a special reception honoring Annie was held in the Ohio Pavilion at the World's Fair in Chicago, Illinois. There Oakley met reporter Amy Leslie, who would become one of her dear friends. Leslie wrote:

> *There is not a nicer wife or woman in the land than Annie Oakley. ... When she was in Europe royalty courted her and she accepted it as she would the complacent attentions of a village quilting party.*

Another reporter asked Oakley what it took to become such an amazing shooter. Oakley responded:

> *I suppose it's a gift, though practice helps. ... Still, I've gone for months without touching a gun, and then stepped into the ring without preliminary practice and made as good a score as I ever did.*

Thomas Alva Edison
(1847–1931) was one
of the world's greatest
inventors. He invented
the phonograph and
improved the lightbulb,
the telephone, and the
telegraph. His kineto-
scope was the forerun-
ner of today's motion
picture camera. In his
film studio, called the
Black Maria, the
first recorded motion
picture was made.
Called Fred Ott's
Sneeze, the film
recorded Fred Ott,
an Edison employee,
sneezing comically.
Edison also filmed acts,
including Annie
Oakley's from Buffalo
Bill's Wild West show.

In April 1894, Oakley's career took a different turn. She became a motion picture star in some of Thomas Edison's first films. Edison wanted to see if his new invention, the kinetoscope motion-picture machine, could follow the flight of a bullet. To his joy, he discovered that not only did it follow Oakley's bullet, but the film also showed the smoke from her rifle and the splintering of the glass balls she shattered.

Crowds waited in line in New York City to be the first to see the 90-second films that featured Oakley. Edison's films were soon being shown in storefront theaters called nickelodeons, where for the price of a nickel, people could watch a film through a kinetoscope. These viewing parlors, also called peep shows, opened in Chicago; Baltimore, Maryland; and Atlantic City, New Jersey. Oakley was becoming more famous as a film star.

By the end of the 1890s, Oakley had grown tired of travel, newspaper interviews, and the constant pressure to perform at her peak night after night in the Wild West show. She wanted more leisure time to

go hunting and stomp through the woods again. But Buffalo Bill depended on her to bring in the crowds. Knowing her value, he made sure to feature Oakley as the star of his show. But in spite of the fame, Oakley thought about quitting.

Life with the show was sometimes difficult. If it rained, the arena could quickly turn to mud. Sawdust

*Footage of one of Edison's first films showed Annie Oakley shooting at a target and then at glass balls thrown into the air by Frank Butler.*

and straw soaked up some of the moisture, but if it rained too hard, the straw didn't help. Oakley said:

> *Women have frequently said to me that I earned my money easily, ... but they only saw the easiest part of my work. They do not think of the times when we would be obliged to "show" in mud ankle deep, and then go to our train drenched to the skin in the storms we encountered. Of course I became accustomed to that sort of thing. One gets used to almost anything in the "show" business.*

The 1901 season was filled with more than the usual hardships. In April, while the troupe was in Washington, D.C., the teepee—the traveling home— of Indian performer One Bear caught fire and burned to the ground. In another tragic accident, a cannon fired too soon, and an injured artilleryman had to have his arm amputated.

Disaster struck again as the troupe traveled to its last show of the season. On the way to Danville, Virginia, their train suddenly saw headlights from an oncoming train. Emergency brakes squealed, but the trains' drivers couldn't avoid a collision. Five of the Wild West's train cars shattered and flew into the ditch. All the horses inside were killed. On the other train, two cars were destroyed. Remarkably, only four people were hurt; one of them was Oakley,

As an entertainer, Annie Oakley lived most of her life in tents while traveling from city to city and country to country with Wild West shows.

who had been sleeping in her stateroom at the time of the crash.

When the trains collided, Oakley was thrown from her bed and hit her back on a trunk. Her injuries were minor—no more than bruises. Within weeks she was back to work. But she didn't return to the Wild West show. Butler sent a letter to Buffalo Bill stating that he and Annie felt it was time to leave. 🝏

# 8 THE HIGH PRICE OF FAME

〜✦〜

Work for 42-year-old Oakley was different now. She began rehearsing for the lead role in the stage play *The Western Girl*. She performed on Broadway in New York City for more than a year as Nancy Barry, a Colorado woman who fought outlaws and rescued innocent people. Audiences were so delighted with her performances that at one showing, Oakley received six curtain calls.

Annie Oakley was famous—for her shooting skills and now for her acting talent. But while some people imitated her, others criticized her. Because she was such an accurate shot, people often claimed that she cheated. Oakley said, "It is all so very easy and simple, and looks it, that the hardest thing in the world ... is to make people believe that there is no

*Annie Oakley gave audiences a taste of the Wild West with her portrayal of a pioneer woman in the stage play* The Western Girl.

cheating." In fact, some shooters did cheat, which was relatively easy to do.

Oakley could shoot the ashes off a cigarette in her assistant's mouth, but this trick could also be done by illusion. Some performers tied a thin piece of clear string to the cigarette. When the shot rang out, the assistants quickly and cleverly pulled the string to make the ashes fall. But Oakley would never resort to cheating. To prove it, she occasionally missed a shot on purpose. She figured people would be less likely to think she cheated if she missed once in a while.

Because Oakley was so famous, people sometimes pretended to be the well-known markswoman. Butler worked hard to stop these imposters and protect his wife's reputation and clean-cut image. He talked to reporters, wrote to newspapers, and confronted these look-alikes face-to-face to put a stop to any lies or rumors.

But as much as Butler tried to protect his wife, many ridiculous newspaper stories were written about her. Sometimes the stories went too far. For the most part, Oakley brushed off made-up stories, but one tale surfaced in 1903 that she couldn't ignore. On August 11, two Chicago newspapers ran articles that claimed she had been thrown into prison after pleading guilty to stealing a pair of pants to pay for her drug habit. To Oakley's horror, the story quickly

*Annie Oakley worked hard to create a clean-cut image and fought hard to uphold her reputation.*

spread to other newspapers across the country.

The woman that the the jailers thought was Oakley was an imposter. But even though the truth came out, the damage had already been done to Oakley's reputation. Oakley was so upset about the whole affair that she said it nearly killed her. "The only thing that kept me alive … was the desire to purge my character," she said.

*Newspapers owned by William Randolph Hearst were the first to print false stories about Annie Oakley.*

The 43-year-old sharpshooter wrote many angry letters to newspapers, including several owned by the newspaper giant William Randolph Hearst. In her letter to the *Philadelphia Press*, she asked the newspaper to print the truth or she would sue for libel, or making false, harmful statements. Some newspapers admitted their mistakes and printed formal statements that took back their previous reports. Some sent personal letters to her, apologizing for their errors. However, Oakley knew all this might go unnoticed by the public.

For the next six years, she filed lawsuits against 55 newspapers for damaging her reputation. She spent most of her time in courtrooms testifying how the articles had harmed her. She traveled across the country at her own expense to make sure the public knew about the mistakes made by these newspapers. Her personal life and career were set aside to ensure she would emerge from the scandal untarnished.

Butler supported his wife through the ordeal. He knew that if people believed the stories originally printed in the newspapers, her reputation would be ruined forever.

During the trials that took place across the country, some lawyers for the newspapers treated her with respect when she spoke. Others weren't so kind. Oakley did not usually let rude defense attorneys rattle her, but on rare occasions, she did. Such was the case in Charleston, South Carolina, when an upset Oakley gave the defense a tongue-lashing. She stated:

> *If the gentlemen who fought for South Carolina during the Civil War conducted their defense with as much cowardice as the defense has been conducted against one little woman in this suit, I don't wonder that they received such a sound thrashing.*

She then told the lawyers she was going to turn around and leave the courtroom right at that moment and added:

> *[This will] give one or all of you gentlemen who are such gallant defenders of a woman's honor a chance to further your cowardice by shooting me in the back if you so chose.*

The name *William Randolph Hearst (1863–1951) has become synonymous with the term yellow journalism. This type of newspaper reporting used sensational and sometimes untrue stories and pictures to increase newspaper sales. By 1935, Hearst owned 30 newspapers, including the San Francisco Examiner, the Chicago Examiner, the Washington Herald, and the New York Daily Mirror. He also owned several magazines, publishing houses, radio stations, and news services.*

In an effort to discredit Oakley before one of the trials, Hearst sent a detective to Greenville to dig up any dirt he could find on her. His detective found nothing. The residents of Greenville, who loved Oakley, were angry that strangers were trying to ruin her good reputation.

Oakley won or settled 54 of the 55 lawsuits she filed. Some of the cases even went to the U.S. Supreme Court, the highest court in the United States. Most of the verdicts awarded Oakley less than $5,000. The largest verdict in her favor was $27,500, which had to be paid by Hearst.

Some people believed Oakley sued the newspapers to make a lot of money. But most people realized her reputation meant more to her than money. The years of courtroom battles were costly for Oakley. She had a lot of travel expenses, and she couldn't make money working while she was preparing her cases and attending court hearings.

Butler also took some time off from work. He and his brother Will collected information for the hearings and investigated details to help Oakley's cases. Oakley was determined to fight every lawsuit through to the finish. She prayed for her name to be cleared, and in the end, she got what she wanted.

Most newspaper reporters believed Oakley had done the right thing, and they stood by her. Once she returned to work, even the newspapers she had defeated in court continued to cover her shooting matches and write flattering stories about her exploits. A reporter for the *Hoboken Observer* in New Jersey sent her a note a few years after she was awarded $3,000 in her case against the newspaper. He wrote:

> Although you dug into us for three thou-
> sand "Iron Men" at a time when three
> thousand was a large sum with us—you
> see we still love you.

Once all the trials were past, Oakley said little about the affair. &

# Women should know how to use Firearms.

## So says Annie Oakley, and at her cosey home in Nutley she illustrates for the benefit of the women of the land the proper way in which to handle deadly weapons

*EXAMINE YOUR FIREARMS CAREFULLY*

Mr. and Mrs. Frank Butler, of Newark, N. J., left November 11 on a week's hunting trip through Sussex and Hunterdon counties. This is their first Jersey gunning trip in several years. Mrs. Butler is better known as Annie Oakley.

*ANNIE OAKLEY GIVING AN EXHIBITION AT HER HOME.*

*"NEVER HOLD A REVOLVER THIS WAY "*

*A REVOLVER SHOULD BE KEPT CONVENIENT TO THE BEDSIDE.*

# 9 FINAL YEARS

❧❧❧

When her trials ended, Annie Oakley, now in her 50s, went back to open-air arena shows. Between 1911 and 1913, she appeared in Vernon Seavers' Young Buffalo Show. She made her final arena appearance at the last show of the season on October 4, 1913, in Marion, Illinois.

Throughout her career, Oakley made a good deal of money, and she never spent it foolishly. She was generous with others, shared her money with those she loved, and gave quietly to charities. Though she and Butler never had any children of their own, Oakley loved sending money and gifts to her nieces and nephews. She was particularly close to her sister Hulda's daughter, Anna Fern, who went with her to the trials and sometimes joined her on tour. To another

*Annie Oakley encouraged women to learn how to properly handle and care for weapons.*

niece, Irene Patterson, she sent monthly packages of money, clothes, and lace. Oakley also loved to make others' dreams come true. She always regretted not being able to go to school herself, and used her money to help other women get an education.

Oakley also was known for giving orphans free tickets to her shows. These passes usually were punched with holes to distinguish them from paid tickets. One fan said the holes made it look as though Oakley had used them in her shooting tricks. The free passes came to be known as "Annie Oakleys." She was also generous with her time. She served as a mentor to young shooters and—with the help of Butler and their new dog, Dave—gave exhibitions to raise money for the Red Cross.

*As part of her exhibition, Oakley shot an apple off the head of her dog, Dave.*

She also offered to form regiments of female sharpshooters during two wars: the Spanish-American War (1898) and World War I (1914–1918).

The first time, her offer was refused by the military, and the second time it was ignored. Yet Oakley wasn't discouraged. In 1917, she volunteered to serve free of charge as an instructor to soldiers preparing to fight in World War I.

When this offer was also turned down, Oakley and Butler joined the National War Work Council of the Young Men's Christian Association (YMCA) and the War Camp Community Service. Paying their own expenses and bringing their own supplies, they gave exhibitions and lectures at Army posts. Although the government hadn't encouraged her to help, the soldiers showed their appreciation with cheers and letters of thanks.

Oakley liked to keep busy. By now, she had earned enough to retire comfortably, but she found that settling down didn't suit her very well. She and Butler had tried being homeowners. Oakley thought she would enjoy living in a real home rather than a tent. In the early 1890s, they had built a home in Nutley, New Jersey. The large, three-story house was a lot of work, however, and Oakley had to

*Although World War I began in 1914, the United States did not enter the war until 1917. After numerous attacks by German submarines on U.S. merchant ships, U.S. President Woodrow Wilson declared war on Germany on April 6, 1917, and on Austria-Hungary in December. In the summer of 1918, about 10,000 U.S. troops per day began arriving in Europe. On November 11, 1918, a ceasefire came into effect, and opposing armies began withdrawing.*

*Alexander Graham Bell's many experiments led to such devices as the telephone, the photophone, and metal detectors.*

rely on servants to take care of it. She was a difficult boss because she liked things done perfectly and in her own particular style. Many servants quit because they got tired of trying to live up to her ideals of perfection. Oakley admitted, "I went all to pieces under the care of a home." In 1904, the Butlers sold the house.

In 1913, the Butlers built another home. This one was on the shore of Chesapeake Bay near Cambridge, Maryland. Oakley thought she could solve one of her housekeeping problems by insisting the house be built without closets. She was more comfortable keeping her clothes and linens in trunks. The land was a hunter's paradise where Annie and Frank hunted and fished in the summers with their dog.

When cold weather arrived, they headed south to resorts. They spent the quail-hunting season in Leesburg, Florida, and the winter months in Pinehurst, North Carolina, where they stayed at the Carolina, the area's finest hotel. It attracted many famous guests, including future president Warren Harding, inventor Alexander Graham Bell, and musician John Philip Sousa. Four stories tall and advanced for its time, the Carolina had elevators, electric lights, and telephones in every room. Oakley gave free shooting lessons to the women who stayed there. She patiently taught them and gave them shooting tips:

> *After mastering the singles you are ready for the double targets. Twin targets are not two birds at the same time but one after the other. Consider only the first target until it is smashed, then give attention to the second. The shooter who thinks about both at once will miss them both.*

The Butlers enjoyed spending time with friends. Among them were comedian and actor Fred Stone and his wife, Allene. The Butlers often visited the

Stones at their home in Amityville, New York. Stone enjoyed introducing Oakley to his other friends and noticing their reactions. He said:

> *It was always amusing to watch people who were meeting her for the first time. ... They expected to see a big, masculine, blustering sort of person, and the tiny woman with the quiet voice took them by surprise. ... There was never a sweeter, gentler, more lovable woman than Annie Oakley.*

*Fred Stone initially made a name for himself as a comedian. He later became famous as the Scarecrow in the 1903 stage production of the Wizard of Oz. Stone and Frank Butler occasionally hunted together, and Butler introduced his new friend to trapshooting.*

On July 1, 1922, Stone organized a circus on Long Island, New York, as a charity event to help raise money for injured soldiers. Oakley and Butler happily agreed to participate. The circus began with a parade led by the Butlers. Behind them were trucks carrying circus equipment and actors who performed as they passed in front of the grandstand.

Now nearly 62 years old and wearing glasses, Oakley showed that she could still wow the crowd with her amazing sharp-shooting skills. The event closed with a re-enactment of a stagecoach attack.

In October of that year, about 100,000 people came to see her perform at a fair in Massachusetts. The following month, the Butlers joined friends on a trip to Florida. As they rode in a chauffeur-driven Cadillac, the trip quickly turned tragic. A passing car forced the Cadillac into the sandy shoulder along the edge of the road. The chauffeur tried to get the car back on the road, but instead, it overturned. Oakley was pinned under the car. When rescuers got her out, they rushed her by ambulance to a hospital in Daytona, Florida, where she faced a long recovery.

*In the summer of 1922, Oakley rode past the grandstand with Fred Stone at the Wild West Circus for Society Folks in New York City.*

Though Oakley's life had been spared, her hip was broken and her right ankle shattered. Her husband refused to leave her. For six weeks, he lived in a room across from the hospital and visited her every day, providing support and encouragement as she recovered.

As her body mended, Oakley received thousands of letters, telegrams, and bouquets of flowers. She began to walk with the aid of crutches and a steel brace that supported her right leg. In time, she would trade the crutches for a cane, but she would never be able to walk again without a steel brace.

*Oakley and Butler posed for a picture with their dog, Dave, in the early 1920s.*

She was still recovering from her injuries when a second tragedy struck. On February 25, 1923, while

Butler and Dave were out for a walk, the dog darted into the street to chase a squirrel. He was hit and killed instantly by a car. To the Butlers, Dave's death was like losing a child. He had traveled everywhere with them, his tricks were part of Oakley's act, and he had helped raise money for the Red Cross. Dave even had his own personalized Christmas card that the Butlers sent to their friends.

Despite her sadness, Oakley forced herself to focus on her recovery. Doctors warned her that she would probably never be steady enough to shoot again, but she intended to prove them wrong. Oakley recovered enough to give more exhibitions and donate her earnings to charity. However, her health continued to decline, and she grew more fragile.

In December 1924, the Butlers traveled to Dayton, Ohio, to be closer to Oakley's family. Butler urged Oakley to write her life story, but it was difficult for her. She got as far as 1890 before quitting. Always modest, she downplayed many of her accomplishments and sometimes confused dates. However, people treasured her stories, which were printed in several newspapers.

In the summer of 1926, Oakley and Butler moved to a farm near Ansonia, Ohio, where they lived with members of Oakley's family. As fall neared, Oakley encouraged Butler to go ahead with their plan to return to Pinehurst, North Carolina, for the winter.

She, however, would stay in Ohio to continue to recuperate. Although Butler wasn't well, he didn't want to upset his sickly wife. He did as she asked.

Butler first traveled to New Jersey for a shooting match. Afterward, he didn't feel well enough to go on to Pinehurst alone. Either he or a friend contacted Butler's relatives in Detroit, Michigan. When they saw he was too ill either to go south or to return to his wife in Ohio, they took him into their home to care for him. Meanwhile, as Oakley's health deteriorated, she realized she needed full-time nursing care and moved to a boardinghouse in Greenville, Ohio. About eight weeks later, at around 11 P.M. on November 3, 1926, 66-year-old Annie Oakley died in her sleep.

Before her death, Oakley had made arrangements for her funeral. She chose a female embalmer because she didn't want a man handling her body. A private funeral was held on November 5, 1926, at the home of Oakley's friends in Greenville. According to Oakley's wishes, her body was cremated in Cincinnati. Her ashes were placed in an oak box and put in a vault at the funeral home.

Because of his poor health, Butler wasn't able to attend the funeral. When he heard about her death, he was devastated. He quit eating, and his health quickly grew worse. On November 21, 18 days after his wife's death, 76-year-old Frank Butler died. Oakley had once said:

*After traveling through fourteen foreign countries and appearing before all the royalty and nobility I have only one wish today. That is that when my eyes are closed in death that they will bury me back in that quiet little farm land where I was born.*

*In 1926, Oakley's and Butler's ashes were buried side by side in Brock Cemetery in western Ohio.*

Oakley got her wish. On Thanksgiving Day 1926, Oakley and Butler were buried next to each other near Greenville in Brock Cemetery. It is just off the western Ohio highway that is now called the Annie Oakley Memorial Pike.

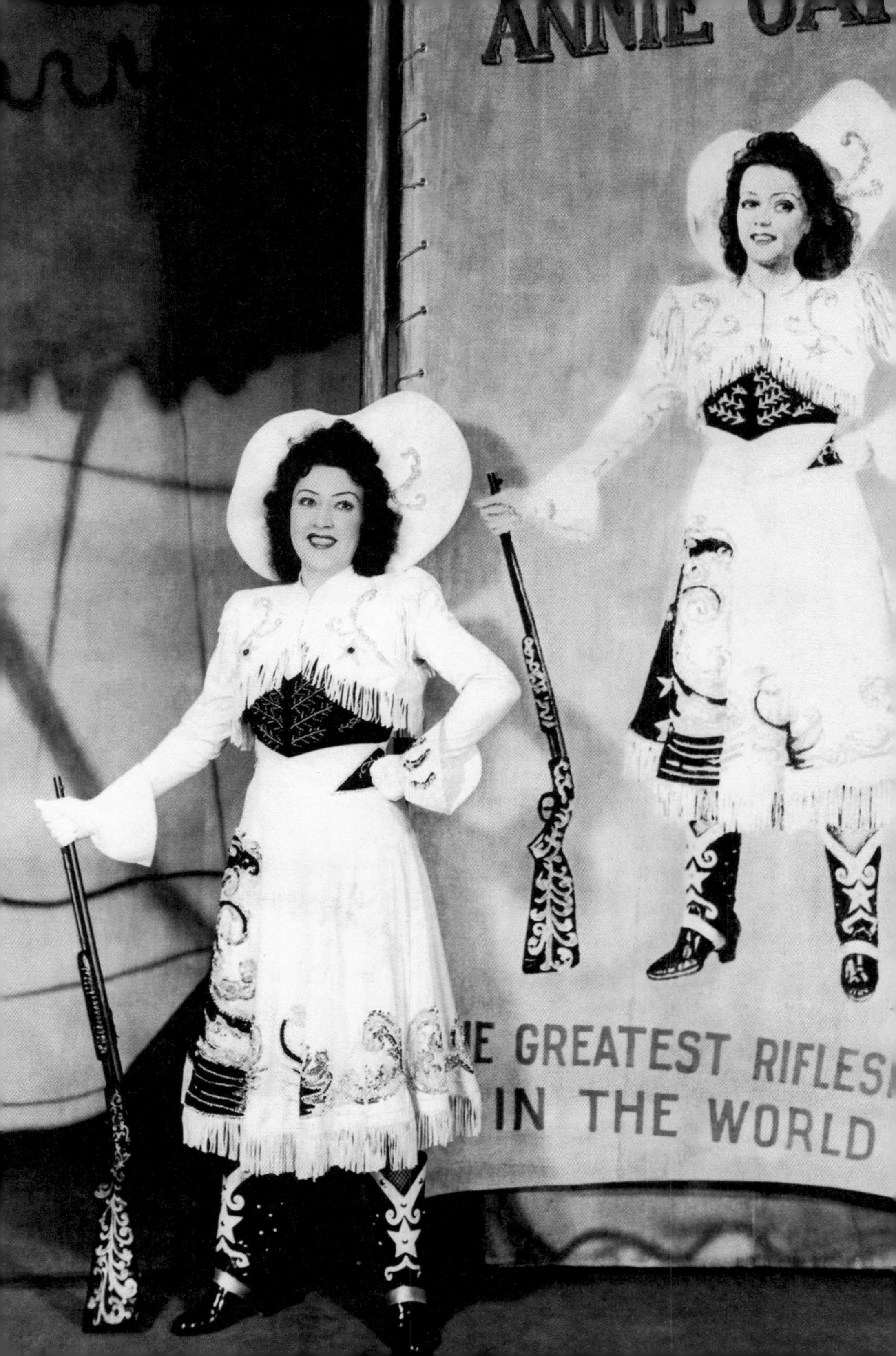
ANNIE
GREATEST
IN THE WORLD

# 10 THE LEGEND OF ANNIE OAKLEY

Even after Oakley's death, many people still admired this great entertainer and markswoman. In the years after her death, Oakley wasn't forgotten. Her legend began to grow. Her life became the subject of newspaper articles, books, museum exhibits, comic books, plays, and movies.

In 1935, actress Barbara Stanwyck played the part of Oakley in a film called *Annie Oakley*. Even though it was a fictional story of Annie's relationship with Frank Butler, it still increased Oakley's legend.

On May 16, 1946, Oakley's story debuted as a Broadway musical at the Imperial Theatre in New York City. Actress and singer Ethel Merman played the part of Annie Oakley in this stage show called *Annie Get Your Gun*. The script didn't always follow

*Ethel Merman starred as Annie Oakley in Irving Berlin's 1946 musical* Annie Get Your Gun.

*Born Ethel Zimmermann in Queens, New York, Ethel Merman (1908–1984) made a name for herself first as a vaudeville performer. Eventually, she appeared on Broadway in New York with a run of 1,147 stage performances. Merman's strong, loud voice and the clearness with which she pronounced the lyrics to her songs helped make her a unique star.*

the facts of Oakley's life, but it still became a hit. Merman's portrayal of Annie Oakley kept Oakley's name in the public eye. Later, the show was turned into a popular movie with the same title.

In 1954, the CBS television network created a program called *Annie Oakley*. The TV show was fictional and didn't follow the facts of Oakley's life. In the series, Oakley lived on a Texas ranch with her brother Tagg. She helped protect the nearby town of Diablo from outlaws with the help of Lofty, the local sheriff, who also served as her love interest. Although the show had little to do with any actual events in Oakley's life, it did expand her legend and depict her true spirit—self-reliant, athletic, competitive, yet feminine. *Annie Oakley* ran for 81 episodes.

Today, Oakley's legend lives on. She continues to be the subject of books, museum exhibits, and Web sites that explore her life. She grew up in Ohio and never lived in the Wild West, but she certainly became a symbol of it. She also became an example of modesty and clean living, while at the same time challenging the traditional roles of men and

*Actress Gail Davis starred in the* Annie Oakley *TV series that premiered January 1, 1954. The final show, titled "Desperate Men," aired February 1, 1957.*

women. She proved that women could do anything they wanted, including hunting and shooting, and still be ladies. She opened doors for other female performers, including those who wanted to join the rodeo circuit.

Annie Oakley began life with a difficult childhood, but she used her skills and talents to succeed. Throughout her career, she worked hard and remained true to herself and her values. "From the time I was nine, I never had a nickel I did not earn myself," a proud Oakley once told a friend. Throughout her life, Oakley lived by her motto:

*A statue of Annie Oakley stands in the Annie Oakley Memorial Park in Greenville, Ohio.*

*Aim at a high mark and you will hit it.
No, not the first time, nor the second and
maybe not the third. But keep on aiming
and keep on shooting for only practice will
make you perfect. Finally, you'll hit the
Bull's-Eye of Success.*

Her motto aptly describes who Annie Oakley was
and how she lived her life.

This master sharpshooter and entertainer known
as Little Sure Shot became an American legend.
Annie Oakley gave the world an admirable example
of determination, independence, values, and strength
of character. ✇

## OAKLEY'S LIFE

### 1860

Born August 13 in
Darke County, Ohio

### 1866

Father, Jacob
Moses, dies

### 1875

Beats Frank
Butler in a
shooting match

## 1860

### 1860

Postage stamps
are widely
used throughout
the world

### 1865

Slavery is abolished
in the United States

### 1875

Russian novelist
Leo Tolstoy's
second masterpiece
*Anna Karenina* is
published in
installments,
ending in 1877; his
epic *War and Peace*
was published
in 1869

## WORLD EVENTS

## 1876

Marries Butler
August 23

## 1882

Takes the
stage with her
husband for
the first time

## 1884

Meets Sitting
Bull; joins Sells
Brothers Circus

## 1880

## 1876

Alexander
Graham Bell
makes the first
successful
telephone
transmission

## 1881

Clara Barton founds
the Red Cross

## 1884

The first practical
fountain pen is
invented by Lewis
Edson Waterman, a
45-year-old American
insurance broker

## OAKLEY'S LIFE

**1885**

Stars in Buffalo
Bill's Wild West
show

**1887**

Travels to
London with
Buffalo Bill's
Wild West; per-
forms in other
European cities

**1889**

Rejoins the
Wild West show

1885

**1886**

Grover Cleveland
dedicates the Statue
of Liberty in New York
Harbor, a gift from the
people of France

**1889**

The Eiffel
Tower opens
in Paris,
France

## WORLD EVENTS

## 1894

Is filmed in
one of Thomas
Edison's first
motion pictures

## 1901

Shaken up in
a train wreck;
quits the Wild
West show

## 1902-03

Plays role of
Nancy Barry in
the Broadway
stage play *The
Western Girl*

## 1900

## 1901

Britain's Queen
Victoria dies

## 1896

The first modern
Olympic Games
are held in
Athens, Greece

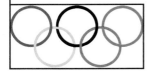

## OAKLEY'S LIFE

### 1903

Begins six-year fight to regain her reputation after newspapers owned by William Randolph Hearst run false stories

### 1911

Joins Young Buffalo show

### 1917

Offers to organize a women's regiment to fight in World War I; gives lectures and exhibitions at Army posts; helps raise money for the Red Cross

## 1910

### 1903

Brothers Orville and Wilbur Wright successfully fly a powered airplane

### 1912

The *Titanic* sinks on its maiden voyage; more than 1,500 people die

### 1917

Vladimir Lenin and Leon Trotsky lead Bolsheviks in a rebellion against the Russian government during the October Revolution

## WORLD EVENTS

**1922**

Injured in
car accident

**1923**

Her beloved dog,
Dave, dies

**1926**

Dies November 3
in Greenville, Ohio;
husband dies 18
days later

1925

**1922**

The tomb of
Tutankhamen
is discovered
by British
archaeologist
Howard Carter

**1923**

Irish Civil War
ends and the
rebels sign a
peace treaty

**1926**

A. A. Milne
publishes
*Winnie the
Pooh*

| | |
|---:|:---|
| **DATE OF BIRTH:** | August 13, 1860 |
| **BIRTHPLACE:** | Darke County, Ohio |
| **FATHER:** | Jacob Moses (1799-1866) |
| **MOTHER:** | Susan Moses (1832-1908) |
| **EDUCATION:** | Little formal education |
| **SPOUSE:** | Frank Butler (1850-1926) |
| **DATE OF MARRIAGE:** | August 23, 1876 |
| **DATE OF DEATH:** | November 3, 1926 |
| **PLACE OF BURIAL:** | Brock Cemetery near Greenville, Ohio |

## FURTHER READING

Flynn, Jean. *Annie Oakley: Legendary Sharpshooter*. Springfield, N.J.: Enslow Publishers, 1998.

Landau, Elaine. *Annie Oakley: Wild West Sharpshooter*. Berkeley Heights, N.J.: Enslow, 2004.

Macy, Sue. *Bull's-Eye: A Photobiography of Annie Oakley*. Washington, D.C.: National Geographic Children's Books, 2006.

Spinner, Stephanie. *Who Was Annie Oakley?* New York: Grosset & Dunlap, 2002.

## LOOK FOR MORE SIGNATURE LIVES
### BOOKS ABOUT THIS ERA:

Clara Barton: *Founder of the American Red Cross*

George Washington Carver: *Scientist, Inventor, and Teacher*

Amelia Earhart: *Legendary Aviator*

Thomas Alva Edison: *Great American Inventor*

Yo-Yo Ma: *Renowned Concert Cellist*

Thurgood Marshall: *Civil Rights Lawyer and Supreme Court Justice*

Will Rogers: *Cowboy, Comedian, and Commentator*

Amy Tan: *Writer and Storyteller*

Madam C.J. Walker: *Entrepreneur and Millionaire*

Booker T. Washington: *Innovative Educator*

## ON THE WEB

For more information on this topic, use
FactHound.

1. Go to *www.facthound.com*
2. Type in this book ID: 0756518695
3. Click on the *Fetch It* button.

FactHound will find the best Web
sites for you.

## HISTORIC SITES

Garst Museum
205 N. Broadway
Greenville, OH 45331
937/548-5250
The Annie Oakley Center shows the life
and times of Annie Oakley and Darke
County, Ohio, where she was born

Buffalo Bill Historical Center
720 Sheridan Ave.
Cody, WY 82414
307/587-4771
Museums, exhibits, and a library of the
people and times of the Wild West

**clay pigeon**
target made of clay used by trapshooters; it
replaced the use of live birds as a cheaper and
more humane alternative

**demeanor**
outward manner or behavior

**frugal**
careful with money

**libel**
published statement or article that gives readers a
false idea about a person

**markswoman**
woman who is able to shoot accurately

**skittish**
easily frightened

**traps**
devices that hurl targets into the air
for trapshooters

**trapshooting**
the sport of shooting at clay pigeons sprung from
a trap into the air

**tuberculosis**
highly contagious disease that affects the lungs

**vaudeville**
stage entertainment composed of a variety of acts
such as acrobats, dancers, and comedians

**Chapter 1**

Page 12, line 13: Glenda Riley. *The Life and Legacy of Annie Oakley.* Norman, OK: University of Oklahoma Press, 1994, p. 90.

**Chapter 2**

Page 17, line 12: Sue Macy. *Bull's-Eye: A Photobiography of Annie Oakley.* Washington, D.C.: National Geographic Society, 2001, p. 16.

Page 19, line 11: *The Life and Legacy of Annie Oakley*, p. 4.

Page 20, line 8: Shirl Kasper. *Annie Oakley.* Norman: University of Oklahoma Press, 1992, p. 4.

Page 20, line 18: Ibid.

**Chapter 3**

Page 25, line 8: *The Life and Legacy of Annie Oakley*, p. 6.

Page 26, line 1: Ibid., p. 7.

Page 27, line 5: Ibid., p. 8.

**Chapter 4**

Page 32, line 13: *Annie Oakley*, p. 17.

**Chapter 5**

Page 39, line 3: Ibid., p. 27.

**Chapter 6**

Page 47, line 2: Candace Savage. *Cowgirls.* Berkeley, Calif.: Ten Speed Press, 1996, p. 52.

Page 47, line 5: Ibid., p. 43.

Page 48, line 9: *The Life and Legacy of Annie Oakley*, p. 31.

Page 51, line 3: *Cowgirls*, p. 47.

**Chapter 7**

Page 58, line 21: *The Life and Legacy of Annie Oakley*, p. 40.

Page 60, line 7: Ibid., p. 140.

Page 61, line 14: *Bull's-Eye: A Photobiography of Annie Oakley*, p. 15.

Page 65, line 15: *Annie Oakley*, p. 126.

Page 65, line 22: Ibid., p. 131.

Page 68, line 3: Ibid., p. 148.

**Chapter 8**

Page 71, line 13: Ibid., p. 47.

Page 74, line 1: *The Life and Legacy of Annie Oakley*, p. 77.

Page 75, line 14: Ibid., p. 80.

Page 77, line 14: Ibid., p. 83.

**Chapter 9**

Page 82, line 5: Ibid., p. 178.

Page 83, line 18: Walter Havighurst. *Annie Oakley and the Wild West.* Edison, N.J.: Castle Books, 2003, p. 218.

Page 84, line 4: *Annie Oakley*, p. 188.

Page 89, line 1: *Bull's-Eye: A Photobiography of Annie Oakley*, p. 56.

**Chapter 10**

Page 93, line 9: *Cowgirls*, p. 43.

Page 95, line 1: The Annie Oakley Foundation, http://www.annieoakleyfoundation.org/bio.html.

"Annie Oakley." *Buffalo Bill Historical Center (2004)*. 30 May 2006.
www.bbhc.org/bbm/biographyAO.cfm

"Annie Oakley." *PBS.org*. 30 May 2006. www.pbs.org/wgbh/amex/oakley

Edwards, Bess. "Annie Oakley's Life and Career." *The Annie Oakley Foundation*. 19 Dec. 2005. 30 May 2006. www.annieoakleyfoundation.org/bio.html

Havighurst, Walter. *Annie Oakley of the Wild West*. Edison, N.J.: Castle Books, 2003.

Kasper, Shirl. *Annie Oakley*. Norman: University of Oklahoma Press, 1992.

Riley, Glenda. *The Life and Legacy of Annie Oakley*. Norman: University of Oklahoma Press, 1994.

Savage, Candace. *Cowgirls*. Berkeley, Calif.: Ten Speed Press, 1996.

Brenda Haugen started in the newspaper business and had a career as an award-winning journalist before finding her niche as an author. Since then, she has written and edited many books, most of them for children. A graduate of the University of North Dakota in Grand Forks, Brenda lives in North Dakota with her family.

## Image Credits